GOOD NEWS
TOLD BY MARK

Today's English Version

THE BIBLE SOCIETIES

COLLINS/FOUNT

© American Bible Society,
New York 1966, 1971, and 4th edition 1976

Permission to reproduce any part of the British Edition
should be requested from:

Bible Society
Stonehill Green, Westlea, SWINDON SN5 7DG

English TEV560P Mark
ISBN 0 564 06771 7
BFBS/NBSS/50M/1988

Printed in Great Britain by
Collins Clear-Type Press, London and Glasgow

The *United Bible Societies* is a world-wide fellowship of national Bible Societies working in more than 180 countries. Their aim is to reach all people with the Bible or some part of it in a language they can understand and at a price they can afford. More than 500 million Scriptures are distributed every year. You are invited to share in this work by your prayers and gifts. The Bible Society in your country will be very happy to provide details of its activity.

THE GOSPEL ACCORDING TO

MARK

INTRODUCTION

The Gospel according to Mark begins with the statement that it is "the Good News about Jesus Christ, the Son of God." Jesus is pictured as a man of action and authority. His authority is seen in his teaching, in his power over demons, and in forgiving people's sins. Jesus speaks of himself as the Son of Man, who came to give his life to set people free from sin.

Mark presents the story of Jesus in a straightforward, vigorous way, with emphasis on what Jesus did, rather than on his words and teachings. After a brief prologue about John the Baptist and the baptism and temptation of Jesus, the writer immediately takes up Jesus' ministry of healing and teaching. As time goes on, the followers of Jesus come to understand him better, but Jesus' opponents become more hostile. The closing chapters report the events of Jesus' last week of earthly life, especially his crucifixion and resurrection.

The two endings to the Gospel, which are enclosed in brackets, are generally regarded as written by someone other than the author of *Mark.*

Outline of Contents

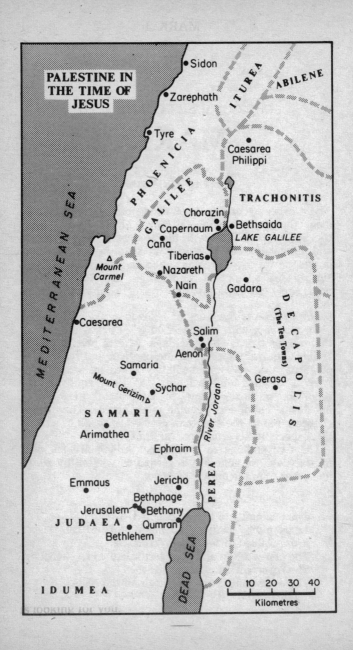

PALESTINE IN THE TIME OF JESUS

MEDITERRANEAN SEA

Sidon
Zarephath
Tyre

PHOENICIA

ITUREA
ABILENE

Caesarea Philippi

GALILEE

TRACHONITIS

Chorazin
Capernaum
Cana
Tiberias
Nazareth
Nain

Bethsaida
LAKE GALILEE

△ Mount Carmel

Gadara

Caesarea

Salim
Aenon

D E C A P O L I S
(The Ten Towns)

Gerasa

Samaria
Mount Gerizim △ Sychar

SAMARIA

Arimathea

Ephraim

River Jordan

PEREA

Emmaus

Jericho
Bethphage
Jerusalem ● Bethany
JUDAEA ● Qumran
Bethlehem

DEAD SEA

IDUMEA

0 10 20 30 40
Kilometres

The Preaching of John the Baptist
(Matt. 3.1–12; Luke 3.1–18; John 1.19–28)

1 This is the Good News about Jesus Christ, the Son of God.[a] [2]It began as the prophet Isaiah had written:

"God said, 'I will send my messenger ahead of you
to clear the way for you.'
[3] Someone is shouting in the desert,
'Get the road ready for the Lord;
make a straight path for him to travel!'"

[4] So John appeared in the desert, baptizing and preaching.[b] "Turn away from your sins and be baptized," he told the people, "and God will forgive your sins." [5]Many people from the province of Judaea and the city of Jerusalem went out to hear John. They confessed their sins, and he baptized them in the River Jordan.

[6] John wore clothes made of camel's hair, with a leather belt round his waist, and his food was locusts and wild honey. [7]He announced to the people, "The man who will come after me is much greater than I am. I am not good enough even to bend down and untie his sandals. [8]I baptize you with water, but he will baptize you with the Holy Spirit."

The Baptism and Temptation of Jesus
(Matt. 3.13—4.11; Luke 3.21–22; 4.1–13)

[9] Not long afterwards Jesus came from Nazareth in the province of Galilee, and was baptized by John in the Jordan. [10]As soon as Jesus came up out of the water, he saw heaven opening and the Spirit coming down on him like a dove. [11]And a voice came from heaven, "You are my own dear Son. I am pleased with you."

[12] At once the Spirit made him go into the desert, [13]where he stayed forty days, being tempted by Satan.

---

[a] *Some manuscripts do not have* the Son of God.
[b] John appeared in the desert, baptizing and preaching; *some manuscripts have* John the Baptist appeared in the desert, preaching.

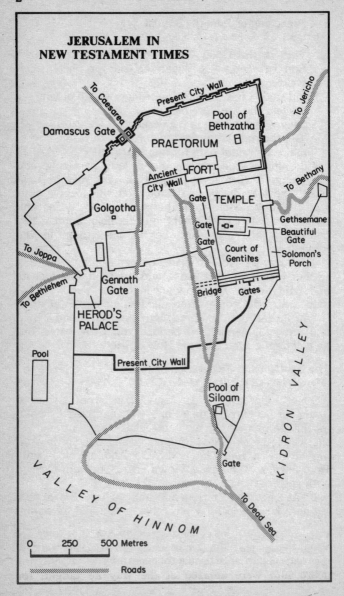

JERUSALEM IN NEW TESTAMENT TIMES

To Caesarea

Present City Wall

To Jericho

Damascus Gate

Pool of Bethzatha

PRAETORIUM

Ancient City Wall

FORT

To Bethany

Gate

TEMPLE

Golgotha

Gethsemane

Beautiful Gate

Gate

Solomon's Porch

Gate

Court of Gentiles

To Joppa

To Bethlehem

Gennath Gate

Bridge

Gates

HEROD'S PALACE

Pool

Present City Wall

Pool of Siloam

KIDRON VALLEY

Gate

VALLEY OF HINNOM

To Dead Sea

0   250   500 Metres

Roads

Wild animals were there also, but angels came and helped him.

Jesus Calls Four Fishermen
(Matt. 4.12–22; Luke 4.14–15; 5.1–11)

14 After John had been put in prison, Jesus went to Galilee and preached the Good News from God. 15 "The right time has come," he said, "and the Kingdom of God is near! Turn away from your sins and believe the Good News!"

16 As Jesus walked along the shore of Lake Galilee, he saw two fishermen, Simon and his brother Andrew, catching fish with a net. 17 Jesus said to them, "Come with me, and I will teach you to catch men." 18 At once

At once they left their nets (1.18)

they left their nets and went with him.

19 He went a little farther on and saw two other brothers, James and John, the sons of Zebedee. They were in their boat getting their nets ready. 20 As soon as Jesus saw them, he called them; they left their father Zebedee in the boat with the hired men and went with Jesus.

A Man with an Evil Spirit
(Luke 4.31–37)

21 Jesus and his disciples came to the town of Capernaum, and on the next Sabbath Jesus went to the synagogue and began to teach. 22 The people who heard him were amazed at the way he taught, for

he wasn't like the teachers of the Law; instead, he taught with authority.

23 Just then a man with an evil spirit in him came into the synagogue and screamed, 24"What do you want with us, Jesus of Nazareth? Are you here to destroy us? I know who you are—you are God's holy messenger!"

25 Jesus ordered the spirit, "Be quiet, and come out of the man!"

26 The evil spirit shook the man hard, gave a loud scream, and came out of him. 27The people were all so amazed that they started saying to one another, "What is this? Is it some kind of new teaching? This man has authority to give orders to the evil spirits, and they obey him!"

28 And so the news about Jesus spread quickly everywhere in the province of Galilee.

Jesus Heals Many People
(Matt. 8.14–17; Luke 4.38–41)

29 Jesus and his disciples, including James and John, left the synagogue and went straight to the home of Simon and Andrew. 30Simon's mother-in-law was sick in bed with a fever, and as soon as Jesus arrived, he was told about her. 31He went to her, took her by the hand, and helped her up. The fever left her, and she began to wait on them.

32 After the sun had set and evening had come, people brought to Jesus all the sick and those who had demons. 33All the people of the town gathered in front of the house. 34Jesus healed many who were sick with all kinds of diseases and drove out many demons. He would not let the demons say anything, because they knew who he was.

Jesus Preaches in Galilee
(Luke 4.42–44)

35 Very early the next morning, long before daylight, Jesus got up and left the house. He went out of the town to a lonely place, where he prayed. 36But Simon and his companions went out searching for him, 37and when they found him, they said, "Everyone is looking for you."

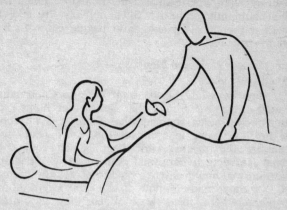

Took her by the hand, and...the fever left her (1.31)

38 But Jesus answered, "We must go on to the other villages round here. I have to preach in them also, because that is why I came."

39 So he travelled all over Galilee, preaching in the synagogues and driving out demons.

Jesus Heals a Man
(Matt. 8.1–4; Luke 5.12–16)

40 A man suffering from a dreaded skin-disease came to Jesus, knelt down, and begged him for help. "If you want to," he said, "you can make me clean."[c]

41 Jesus was filled with pity,[d] and stretched out his hand and touched him. "I do want to," he answered. "Be clean!" 42 At once the disease left the man, and he was clean. 43 Then Jesus spoke sternly to him and sent him away at once, 44 after saying to him, "Listen, don't tell anyone about this. But go straight to the priest and let him examine you; then in order to prove to everyone that you are cured, offer the sacrifice that Moses ordered."

45 But the man went away and began to spread

[c]MAKE ME CLEAN: *This disease was considered to make a person ritually unclean.*   [d]pity; *some manuscripts have* anger.

the news everywhere. Indeed, he talked so much that Jesus could not go into a town publicly. Instead, he stayed out in lonely places, and people came to him from everywhere.

Jesus Heals a Paralysed Man
(Matt. 9.1–8; Luke 5.17–26)

2 A few days later Jesus went back to Capernaum, and the news spread that he was at home. ²So many people came together that there was no room left, not even out in front of the door. Jesus was preaching the message to them ³when four men arrived, carrying a paralysed man to Jesus. ⁴Because of the crowd, however, they could not get the man to him. So they made a hole in the roof right above the place where Jesus was. When they had made an opening, they let the man down, lying on his mat. ⁵Seeing how much faith they had, Jesus said to the paralysed man, "My son, your sins are forgiven."

6 Some teachers of the Law who were sitting there thought to themselves, ⁷"How does he dare to talk like this? This is blasphemy! God is the only one who can forgive sins!"

8 At once Jesus knew what they were thinking, so he said to them, "Why do you think such things? ⁹Is it easier to say to this paralysed man, 'Your sins are forgiven', or to say, 'Get up, pick up your mat, and walk'? ¹⁰I will prove to you, then, that the Son of Man has authority on earth to forgive sins." So he said to the paralysed man, ¹¹"I tell you, get up, pick up your mat, and go home!"

12 While they all watched, the man got up, picked up his mat, and hurried away. They were all completely amazed and praised God, saying, "We have never seen anything like this!"

Jesus Calls Levi
(Matt. 9.9–13; Luke 5.27–32)

13 Jesus went back again to the shore of Lake Galilee. A crowd came to him, and he started teaching them. ¹⁴As he walked along, he saw a tax collector, Levi son of Alphaeus, sitting in his office. Jesus said to him, "Follow me." Levi got up and followed him.

15 Later on Jesus was having a meal in Levi's
house.ᵉ A large number of tax collectors and other
outcasts were following Jesus, and many of them joined
him and his disciples at the table. 16 Some teachers of
the Law, who were Pharisees, saw that Jesus was
eating with these outcasts and tax collectors, so they
asked his disciples, "Why does he eat with such
people?"

17 Jesus heard them and answered, "People who
are well do not need a doctor, but only those who
are sick. I have not come to call respectable people,
but outcasts."

The Question about Fasting
(Matt. 9.14–17; Luke 5.33–39)

18 On one occasion the followers of John the Baptist
and the Pharisees were fasting. Some people came
to Jesus and asked him, "Why is it that the disciples
of John the Baptist and the disciples of the Pharisees
fast, but yours do not?"

19 Jesus answered, "Do you expect the guests at
a wedding party to go without food? Of course not!
As long as the bridegroom is with them, they will
not do that. 20 But the day will come when the bridegroom will be taken away from them, and then they
will fast.

21 "No one uses a piece of new cloth to patch
up an old coat, because the new patch will shrink
and tear off some of the old cloth, making an even
bigger hole. 22 Nor does anyone pour new wine into
used wineskins, because the wine will burst the skins,
and both the wine and the skins will be ruined. Instead,
new wine must be poured into fresh wineskins."

The Question about the Sabbath
(Matt. 12.1–8; Luke 6.1–5)

23 Jesus was walking through some cornfields on
the Sabbath. As his disciples walked along with him,
they began to pick the ears of corn. 24 So the Pharisees
said to Jesus, "Look, it is against our Law for your
disciples to do that on the Sabbath!"

ᵉin Levi's house; *or* in his (*that is,* Jesus') house.

25 Jesus answered, "Have you never read what
David did that time when he needed something to
eat? He and his men were hungry, 26 so he went into
the house of God and ate the bread offered to God.
This happened when Abiathar was the High Priest.
According to our Law only the priests may eat this
bread—but David ate it and even gave it to his men."

27 And Jesus concluded, "The Sabbath was made
for the good of man; man was not made for the
Sabbath. 28 So the Son of Man is Lord even of the
Sabbath."

The Man with a Paralysed Hand
(Matt. 12.9-14; Luke 6.6-11)

3 Then Jesus went back to the synagogue, where
there was a man who had a paralysed hand. 2 Some
people were there who wanted to accuse Jesus of
doing wrong; so they watched him closely to see
whether he would heal the man on the Sabbath. 3 Jesus
said to the man, "Come up here to the front." 4 Then
he asked the people, "What does our Law allow us
to do on the Sabbath? To help or to harm? To save
a man's life or to destroy it?"

But they did not say a thing. 5 Jesus was angry
as he looked round at them, but at the same time
he felt sorry for them, because they were so stubborn
and wrong. Then he said to the man, "Stretch out
your hand." He stretched it out, and it became well
again. 6 So the Pharisees left the synagogue and met
at once with some members of Herod's party, and they
made plans to kill Jesus.

A Crowd by the Lake

7 Jesus and his disciples went away to Lake Galilee,
and a large crowd followed him. They had come from
Galilee, from Judaea, 8 from Jerusalem, from the territory of Idumea, from the territory on the east side
of the Jordan, and from the region round the cities
of Tyre and Sidon. All these people came to Jesus
because they had heard of the things he was doing.
9 The crowd was so large that Jesus told his disciples
to get a boat ready for him, so that the people would
not crush him. 10 He had healed many people, and

The crowd was so large (3.9)

all those who were ill kept pushing their way to him in order to touch him. ¹¹ And whenever the people who had evil spirits in them saw him, they would fall down before him and scream, "You are the Son of God!"

12 Jesus sternly ordered the evil spirits not to tell anyone who he was.

Jesus Chooses the Twelve Apostles
(Matt. 10.1–4; Luke 6.12–16)

13 Then Jesus went up a hill and called to himself the men he wanted. They came to him, ¹⁴ and he chose twelve, whom he named apostles. "I have chosen you to be with me," he told them. "I will also send you out to preach, ¹⁵ and you will have authority to drive out demons."

16 These are the twelve he chose: Simon (Jesus gave him the name Peter); ¹⁷ James and his brother John, the sons of Zebedee (Jesus gave them the name Boanerges, which means "Men of Thunder"); ¹⁸ Andrew, Philip, Bartholomew, Matthew, Thomas,

James son of Alphaeus, Thaddaeus, Simon the Patriot, ¹⁹and Judas Iscariot, who betrayed Jesus.

Jesus and Beelzebul
(Matt. 12.22–32; Luke 11.14–23; 12.10)

20 Then Jesus went home. Again such a large crowd gathered that Jesus and his disciples had no time to eat. ²¹When his family heard about it, they set out to take charge of him, because people were saying, "He's gone mad!"

22 Some teachers of the Law who had come from Jerusalem were saying, "He has Beelzebul in him! It is the chief of the demons who gives him the power to drive them out."

23 So Jesus called them to him and spoke to them in parables: "How can Satan drive out Satan? ²⁴If a country divides itself into groups which fight each other, that country will fall apart. ²⁵If a family divides itself into groups which fight each other, that family will fall apart. ²⁶So if Satan's kingdom divides into groups, it cannot last, but will fall apart and come to an end.

27 "No one can break into a strong man's house and take away his belongings unless he first ties up the strong man; then he can plunder his house.

28 "I assure you that people can be forgiven all their sins and all the evil things they may say.ᶠ ²⁹But whoever says evil things against the Holy Spirit will never be forgiven, because he has committed an eternal sin." ³⁰(Jesus said this because some people were saying, "He has an evil spirit in him.")

Jesus' Mother and Brothers
(Matt. 12.46–50; Luke 8.19–21)

31 Then Jesus' mother and brothers arrived. They stood outside the house and sent in a message, asking for him. ³²A crowd was sitting round Jesus, and they said to him, "Look, your mother and your brothers and sisters are outside, and they want you."

33 Jesus answered, "Who is my mother? Who are

ᶠevil things they may say; *or* evil things they may say against God.

my brothers?" ³⁴He looked at the people sitting round
him and said, "Look! Here are my mother and my
brothers! ³⁵Whoever does what God wants him to
do is my brother, my sister, my mother."

The Parable of the Sower
(Matt. 13.1–9; Luke 8.4–8)

4 Again Jesus began to teach beside Lake Galilee.
The crowd that gathered round him was so large
that he got into a boat and sat in it. The boat was
out in the water, and the crowd stood on the shore
at the water's edge. ²He used parables to teach them
many things, saying to them:

3 "Listen! Once there was a man who went out
to sow corn. ⁴As he scattered the seed in the field,
some of it fell along the path, and the birds came
and ate it up. ⁵Some of it fell on rocky ground,
where there was little soil. The seeds soon sprouted,
because the soil wasn't deep. ⁶Then, when the sun
came up, it burnt the young plants; and because the
roots had not grown deep enough, the plants soon
dried up. ⁷Some of the seed fell among thorn bushes,
which grew up and choked the plants, and they didn't
produce any corn. ⁸But some seeds fell in good soil, and
the plants sprouted, grew, and produced corn: some
had thirty grains, others sixty, and others a hundred."

9 And Jesus concluded, "Listen, then, if you have
ears!"

The Purpose of the Parables
(Matt. 13.10–17; Luke 8.9–10)

10 When Jesus was alone, some of those who had
heard him came to him with the twelve disciples
and asked him to explain the parables. ¹¹"You have
been given the secret of the Kingdom of God," Jesus
answered. "But the others, who are on the outside,
hear all things by means of parables, ¹²so that,
   'They may look and look,
      yet not see;
   they may listen and listen,
      yet not understand.
   For if they did, they would turn to God,
      and he would forgive them.' "

Jesus Explains the Parable of the Sower
(Matt. 13.18-23; Luke 8.11-15)

13 Then Jesus asked them, "Don't you understand this parable? How, then, will you ever understand any parable? 14 The sower sows God's message. 15 Some people are like the seeds that fall along the path; as soon as they hear the message, Satan comes and takes it away. 16 Other people are like the seeds that fall on rocky ground. As soon as they hear the message, they receive it gladly. 17 But it does not sink deep into them, and they don't last long. So when trouble or persecution comes because of the message, they give up at once. 18 Other people are like the seeds sown among the thorn bushes. These are the ones who hear the message, 19 but the worries about this life, the love for riches, and all other kinds of desires crowd in and choke the message, and they don't bear fruit. 20 But other people are like the seeds sown in good soil. They hear the message, accept it, and bear fruit: some thirty, some sixty, and some a hundred."

A Lamp under a Bowl
(Luke 8.16-18)

21 Jesus continued, "Does anyone ever bring in a lamp and put it under a bowl or under the bed? Doesn't he put it on the lampstand? 22 Whatever is hidden away will be brought out into the open, and whatever is covered up will be uncovered. 23 Listen, then, if you have ears!"

24 He also said to them, "Pay attention to what you hear! The same rules you use to judge others will be used by God to judge you—but with even greater severity. 25 The person who has something will be given more, and the person who has nothing will have taken away from him even the little he has."

The Parable of the Growing Seed

26 Jesus went on to say, "The Kingdom of God is like this. A man scatters seed in his field. 27 He sleeps at night, is up and about during the day, and all the while the seeds are sprouting and growing. Yet he does not know how it happens. 28 The soil itself

makes the plants grow and bear fruit; first the tender stalk appears, then the ear, and finally the ear full of corn. 29 When the corn is ripe, the man starts cutting it with his sickle, because harvest time has come.

The Parable of the Mustard Seed
(Matt. 13.31–32, 34; Luke 13.18–19)

30 "What shall we say the Kingdom of God is like?" asked Jesus. "What parable shall we use to explain it? 31 It is like this. A man takes a mustard seed, the smallest seed in the world, and plants it in the ground. 32 After a while it grows up and becomes the biggest of all plants. It puts out such large branches that the birds come and make their nests in its shade."

33 Jesus preached his message to the people, using many other parables like these; he told them as much as they could understand. 34 He would not speak to them without using parables, but when he was alone with his disciples, he would explain everything to them.

Jesus Calms a Storm
(Matt. 8.23–27; Luke 8.22–25)

35 On the evening of that same day Jesus said to his disciples, "Let us go across to the other side of the lake." 36 So they left the crowd; the disciples got into the boat in which Jesus was already sitting, and they took him with them. Other boats were there too. 37 Suddenly a strong wind blew up, and the waves began to spill over into the boat, so that it was about to fill with water. 38 Jesus was in the back of the boat, sleeping with his head on a pillow. The disciples woke him up and said, "Teacher, don't you care that we are about to die?"

39 Jesus stood up and commanded the wind, "Be quiet!" and he said to the waves, "Be still!" The wind died down, and there was a great calm. 40 Then Jesus said to his disciples, "Why are you frightened? Have you still no faith?"

41 But they were terribly afraid and said to one another, "Who is this man? Even the wind and the waves obey him!"

Waves began to spill over into the boat (4.37)

Jesus Heals a Man with Evil Spirits
(Matt. 8.28–34; Luke 8.26–39)

5 Jesus and his disciples arrived on the other side of Lake Galilee, in the territory of Gerasa. ²As soon as Jesus got out of the boat, he was met by a man who came out of the burial caves there. This man had an evil spirit in him ³and lived among the

And there was a great calm (4.39)

tombs. Nobody could keep him chained up any more; [4]many times his feet and hands had been chained, but every time he broke the chains and smashed the irons on his feet. He was too strong for anyone to control him. [5]Day and night he wandered among the tombs and through the hills, screaming and cutting himself with stones.

6 He was some distance away when he saw Jesus; so he ran, fell on his knees before him, [7]and screamed in a loud voice, "Jesus, Son of the Most High God! What do you want with me? For God's sake, I beg you, don't punish me!" [8](He said this because Jesus was saying, "Evil spirit, come out of this man!")

9 So Jesus asked him, "What is your name?"

The man answered, "My name is 'Mob'—there are so many of us!" [10]And he kept begging Jesus not to send the evil spirits out of that region.

11 There was a large herd of pigs near by, feeding on a hillside. [12]So the spirits begged Jesus, "Send us to the pigs, and let us go into them." [13]He let them go, and the evil spirits went out of the man and entered the pigs. The whole herd—about two thousand pigs in all—rushed down the side of the cliff into the lake and was drowned.

14 The men who had been taking care of the pigs ran away and spread the news in the town and among the farms. People went out to see what had happened, [15]and when they came to Jesus, they saw the man who used to have the mob of demons in him. He was sitting there, clothed and in his right mind; and they were all afraid. [16]Those who had seen it told the people what had happened to the man with the demons, and about the pigs.

17 So they asked Jesus to leave their territory.

18 As Jesus was getting into the boat, the man who had had the demons begged him, "Let me go with you!"

19 But Jesus would not let him. Instead, he told him, "Go back home to your family and tell them how much the Lord has done for you and how kind he has been to you."

20 So the man left and went all through the Ten

Towns, telling what Jesus had done for him. And all who heard it were amazed.

Jairus' Daughter and the Woman
Who Touched Jesus' Cloak
(Matt. 9.18–26; Luke 8.40–56)

21 Jesus went back across to the other side of the lake. There at the lakeside a large crowd gathered round him. ²²Jairus, an official of the local synagogue, arrived, and when he saw Jesus, he threw himself down at his feet ²³and begged him earnestly, "My little daughter is very ill. Please come and place your hands on her, so that she will get well and live!"

24 Then Jesus started off with him. So many people were going along with Jesus that they were crowding him from every side.

25 There was a woman who had suffered terribly from severe bleeding for twelve years, ²⁶even though she had been treated by many doctors. She had spent all her money, but instead of getting better she got worse all the time. ²⁷She had heard about Jesus, so she came in the crowd behind him, ²⁸saying to herself, "If I just touch his clothes, I will get well."

29 She touched his cloak, and her bleeding stopped at once; and she had the feeling inside herself that she was healed of her trouble. ³⁰At once Jesus knew that power had gone out of him, so he turned round in the crowd and asked, "Who touched my clothes?"

31 His disciples answered, "You see how the people are crowding you; why do you ask who touched you?"

32 But Jesus kept looking round to see who had done it. ³³The woman realized what had happened to her, so she came, trembling with fear, knelt at his feet, and told him the whole truth. ³⁴Jesus said to her, "My daughter, your faith has made you well. Go in peace, and be healed of your trouble."

35 While Jesus was saying this, some messengers came from Jairus' house and told him, "Your daughter has died. Why bother the Teacher any longer?"

36 Jesus paid no attention to[g] what they said, but told him, "Don't be afraid, only believe." ³⁷Then he

[g] paid no attention to; or overheard.

did not let anyone else go on with him except Peter and James and his brother John. ³⁸They arrived at Jairus' house, where Jesus saw the confusion and heard all the loud crying and wailing. ³⁹He went in and said to them, "Why all this confusion? Why are you crying? The child is not dead—she is only sleeping!"

40 They laughed at him, so he put them all out, took the child's father and mother and his three disciples, and went into the room where the child was lying. ⁴¹He took her by the hand and said to her, "*Talitha, koum*," which means, "Little girl, I tell you to get up!"

42 She got up at once and started walking around. (She was twelve years old.) When this happened, they were completely amazed. ⁴³But Jesus gave them strict orders not to tell anyone, and he said, "Give her something to eat."

Jesus Is Rejected at Nazareth
(Matt. 13.53–58; Luke 4.16–30)

6 Jesus left that place and went back to his home town, followed by his disciples. ²On the Sabbath he began to teach in the synagogue. Many people were there; and when they heard him, they were all amazed. "Where did he get all this?" they asked. "What wisdom is this that has been given him? How does he perform miracles? ³Isn't he the carpenter, the son of Mary, and the brother of James, Joseph, Judas, and Simon? Aren't his sisters living here?" And so they rejected him.

4 Jesus said to them, "A prophet is respected everywhere except in his own home town and by his relatives and his family."

5 He was not able to perform any miracles there, except that he placed his hands on a few sick people and healed them. ⁶He was greatly surprised, because the people did not have faith.

Jesus Sends out the Twelve Disciples
(Matt. 10.5–15; Luke 9.1–6)

Then Jesus went to the villages round there, teaching the people. ⁷He called the twelve disciples together and sent them out two by two. He gave them authority over the evil spirits 8 and ordered them, "Don't take anything with you on your journey except a stick—no bread, no beggar's bag, no money in your pockets. 9 Wear sandals, but don't carry an extra shirt." 10 He also said, "Wherever you are welcomed, stay in the same house until you leave that place. 11 If you come to a town where people do not welcome you or will not listen to you, leave it and shake the dust off your feet. That will be a warning to them!"

12 So they went out and preached that people should turn away from their sins. 13 They drove out many demons, and rubbed olive-oil on many sick people and healed them.

The Death of John the Baptist
(Matt. 14.1-12; Luke 9.7-9)

14 Now King Herod^h heard about all this, because Jesus' reputation had spread everywhere. Some people were saying, "John the Baptist has come back to life! That is why he has this power to perform miracles."

15 Others, however, said, "He is Elijah."

Others said, "He is a prophet, like one of the prophets of long ago."

16 When Herod heard it, he said, "He is John the Baptist! I had his head cut off, but he has come back to life!" 17 Herod himself had ordered John's arrest, and he had him chained and put in prison. Herod did this because of Herodias, whom he had married, even though she was the wife of his brother Philip. 18 John the Baptist kept telling Herod, "It isn't right for you to be married to your brother's wife!"

19 So Herodias held a grudge against John and wanted to kill him, but she could not because of Herod. 20 Herod was afraid of John because he knew that John was a good and holy man, and so he kept him safe. He liked to listen to him, even though he became greatly disturbed every time he heard him.

21 Finally Herodias got her chance. It was on Herod's birthday, when he gave a feast for all the chief govern-

^{h}KING HEROD: *Herod Antipas, ruler of Galilee.*

ment officials, the military commanders, and the leading citizens of Galilee. 22 The daughter of Herodias*i* came in and danced, and pleased Herod and his guests. So the king said to the girl, "What would you like to have? I will give you anything you want." 23 With many vows he said to her, "I swear that I will give you anything you ask for, even as much as half my kingdom!"

24 So the girl went out and asked her mother, "What shall I ask for?"

"The head of John the Baptist," she answered.

25 The girl hurried back at once to the king and demanded, "I want you to give me here and now the head of John the Baptist on a dish!"

26 This made the king very sad, but he could not refuse her because of the vows he had made in front of all his guests. 27 So he sent off a guard at once with orders to bring John's head. The guard left, went to the prison, and cut John's head off; 28 then he brought it on a dish and gave it to the girl, who gave it to her mother. 29 When John's disciples heard about this, they came and took away his body, and buried it.

Jesus Feeds Five Thousand Men
(Matt. 14.13–21; Luke 9.10–17; John 6.1–14)

30 The apostles returned and met with Jesus, and told him all they had done and taught. 31 There were so many people coming and going that Jesus and his disciples didn't even have time to eat. So he said to them, "Let us go off by ourselves to some place where we will be alone and you can rest for a while." 32 So they started out in a boat by themselves for a lonely place.

33 Many people, however, saw them leave and knew at once who they were; so they went from all the towns and ran ahead by land and arrived at the place ahead of Jesus and his disciples. 34 When Jesus got out of the boat, he saw this large crowd, and his heart was filled with pity for them, because they

---

*i*The daughter of Herodias; *some manuscripts have* His daughter Herodias.

were like sheep without a shepherd. So he began to teach them many things. 35 When it was getting late, his disciples came to him and said, "It is already very late, and this is a lonely place. 36 Send the people away, and let them go to the nearby farms and villages in order to buy themselves something to eat."

37 "You yourselves give them something to eat," Jesus answered.

They asked, "Do you want us to go and spend two hundred silver coins*j* on bread in order to feed them?"

38 So Jesus asked them, "How much bread have you got? Go and see."

When they found out, they told him, "Five loaves and also two fish."

39 Jesus then told his disciples to make all the people divide into groups and sit down on the green grass. 40 So the people sat down in rows, in groups of a hundred and groups of fifty. 41 Then Jesus took the five loaves and the two fish, looked up to heaven, and gave thanks to God. He broke the loaves and gave them to his disciples to distribute to the people. He also divided the two fish among them all. 42 Everyone ate and had enough. 43 Then the disciples took up twelve baskets full of what was left of the bread and the fish. 44 The number of men who were fed was five thousand.

Jesus Walks on the Water
(Matt. 14.22–33; John 6.15–21)

45 At once Jesus made his disciples get into the boat and go ahead of him to Bethsaida, on the other side of the lake, while he sent the crowd away. 46 After saying good-bye to the people he went away to a hill to pray. 47 When evening came, the boat was in the middle of the lake, while Jesus was alone on land. 48 He saw that his disciples were straining at the oars, because they were rowing against the wind; so some time between three and six o'clock in the morning he came to them, walking on the water.

j SILVER COINS: *A silver coin was the daily wage of a rural worker (see Mt 20.2).*

It's a ghost! (6.49)

He was going to pass them by,[k] 49 but they saw him
walking on the water. "It's a ghost!" they thought,
and screamed. 50 They were all terrified when they
saw him.

Jesus spoke to them at once, "Courage!" he said.
"It is I. Don't be afraid!" 51 Then he got into the
boat with them, and the wind died down. The disciples
were completely amazed, 52 because they had not under-
stood the real meaning of the feeding of the five
thousand; their minds could not grasp it.

Jesus Heals the Sick in Gennesaret
(Matt. 14.34–36)

53 They crossed the lake and came to land at
Gennesaret, where they tied up the boat. 54 As they
left the boat, people recognized Jesus at once. 55 So
they ran throughout the whole region; and wherever
they heard he was, they brought to him sick people
lying on their mats. 56 And everywhere Jesus went,
to villages, towns, or farms, people would take those
who were ill to the market places and beg him to

[k] pass them by; *or* join them.

let them at least touch the edge of his cloak; and all who touched it were made well.

The Teaching of the Ancestors
(Matt. 15.1–9)

7 Some Pharisees and teachers of the Law who had come from Jerusalem gathered round Jesus. 2 They noticed that some of his disciples were eating their food with hands that were ritually unclean—that is, they had not washed them in the way the Pharisees said people should.

3 (For the Pharisees, as well as the rest of the Jews, follow the teaching they received from their ancestors: they do not eat unless they wash their hands in the proper way; 4 nor do they eat anything that comes from the market unless they wash it first.[l] And they follow many other rules which they have received, such as the proper way to wash cups, pots, copper bowls, and beds. [m])

5 So the Pharisees and the teachers of the Law asked Jesus, "Why is it that your disciples do not follow the teaching handed down by our ancestors, but instead eat with ritually unclean hands?"

6 Jesus answered them, "How right Isaiah was when he prophesied about you! You are hypocrites, just as he wrote:

'These people, says God, honour me with their words,
   but their heart is really far away from me.
7 It is no use for them to worship me,
   because they teach man-made rules
   as though they were God's laws!'

8 "You put aside God's command and obey the teachings of men."

9 And Jesus continued, "You have a clever way of rejecting God's law in order to uphold your own teaching. 10 For Moses commanded, 'Respect your father and your mother,' and, 'Whoever curses his father or his mother is to be put to death.' 11 But

---

[l] anything that comes from the market unless they wash it first; or anything after they come from the market unless they wash themselves first.
[m] Some manuscripts do not have and beds.

you teach that if a person has something he could use to help his father or mother, but says, 'This is Corban' (which means, it belongs to God), [12] he is excused from helping his father or mother. [13] In this way the teaching you pass on to others cancels out the word of God. And there are many other things like this that you do."

The Things that Make a Person Unclean
(Matt. 15.10–20)

14 Then Jesus called the crowd to him once more and said to them, "Listen to me, all of you, and understand. [15] There is nothing that goes into a person from the outside which can make him ritually unclean. Rather, it is what comes out of a person that makes him unclean." [n]

17 When he left the crowd and went into the house, his disciples asked him to explain this saying. [18] "You are no more intelligent than the others," Jesus said to them. "Don't you understand? Nothing that goes into a person from the outside can really make him unclean, [19] because it does not go into his heart but into his stomach and then goes on out of the body." (In saying this, Jesus declared that all foods are fit to be eaten.)

20 And he went on to say, "It is what comes out of a person that makes him unclean. [21] For from the inside, from a person's heart, come the evil ideas which lead him to do immoral things, to rob, kill, [22] commit adultery, be greedy, and do all sorts of evil things; deceit, indecency, jealousy, slander, pride, and folly—[23] all these evil things come from inside a person and make him unclean."

A Woman's Faith
(Matt. 15.21–28)

24 Then Jesus left and went away to the territory near the city of Tyre. He went into a house and did not want anyone to know he was there, but he could not stay hidden. [25] A woman, whose daughter

---

[n] *Some manuscripts add verse 16:* Listen, then, if you have ears! *(see 4.23).*

had an evil spirit in her, heard about Jesus and came
to him at once and fell at his feet. 26The woman
was a Gentile, born in the region of Phoenicia in
Syria. She begged Jesus to drive the demon out of
her daughter. 27But Jesus answered, "Let us first feed
the children. It isn't right to take the children's food
and throw it to the dogs."

28 "Sir," she answered, "even the dogs under the
table eat the children's leftovers!"

29 So Jesus said to her, "Because of that answer,
go back home, where you will find that the demon
has gone out of your daughter!"

30 She went home and found her child lying on
the bed; the demon had indeed gone out of her.

Jesus Heals a Deaf-Mute

31 Jesus then left the neighbourhood of Tyre and
went on through Sidon to Lake Galilee, going by way
of the territory of the Ten Towns. 32Some people
brought him a man who was deaf and could hardly
speak, and they begged Jesus to place his hands on
him. 33So Jesus took him off alone, away from the
crowd, put his fingers in the man's ears, spat, and
touched the man's tongue. 34Then Jesus looked up
to heaven, gave a deep groan, and said to the man,
"*Ephphatha*," which means, "Open up!"

35 At once the man was able to hear, his speech
impediment was removed, and he began to talk without
any trouble. 36Then Jesus ordered the people not to
speak of it to anyone; but the more he ordered them
not to, the more they spoke. 37And all who heard
were completely amazed. "How well he does everything!" they exclaimed. "He even causes the deaf
to hear and the dumb to speak!"

Jesus Feeds Four Thousand People
(Matt. 15.32–39)

8 Not long afterwards another large crowd came
together. When the people had nothing left to
eat, Jesus called the disciples to him and said, 2"I
feel sorry for these people, because they have been
with me for three days and now have nothing to
eat. 3If I send them home without feeding them, they

will faint as they go, because some of them have
come a long way."

4 His disciples asked him, "Where in this desert
can anyone find enough food to feed all these people?"

5 "How much bread have you got?" Jesus asked.

"Seven loaves," they answered.

6 He ordered the crowd to sit down on the ground.
Then he took the seven loaves, gave thanks to God,
broke them, and gave them to his disciples to distribute
to the crowd; and the disciples did so. 7 They also had
a few small fish. Jesus gave thanks for these and
told the disciples to distribute them too. 8-9 Everybody
ate and had enough—there were about four thousand
people. Then the disciples took up seven baskets full
of pieces left over. Jesus sent the people away 10 and
at once got into a boat with his disciples and went
to the district of Dalmanutha.

The Pharisees Ask for a Miracle
(Matt. 16.1-4)

11 Some Pharisees came to Jesus and started to
argue with him. They wanted to trap him, so they
asked him to perform a miracle to show that God
approved of him. 12 But Jesus gave a deep groan and
said, "Why do the people of this day ask for a miracle?
No, I tell you! No such proof will be given to these
people!"

13 He left them, got back into the boat, and started
across to the other side of the lake.

The Yeast of the Pharisees and of Herod
(Matt. 16.5-12)

14 The disciples had forgotten to bring enough bread
and had only one loaf with them in the boat. 15 "Take
care," Jesus warned them, "and be on your guard
against the yeast of the Pharisees and the yeast of
Herod."

16 They started discussing among themselves: "He
says this because we haven't any bread."

17 Jesus knew what they were saying, so he asked
them, "Why are you discussing about not having any
bread? Don't you know or understand yet? Are your
minds so dull? 18 You have eyes—can't you see? You

have ears—can't you hear? Don't you remember
¹⁹when I broke the five loaves for the five thousand
people? How many baskets full of leftover pieces did
you take up?"

"Twelve," they answered.

20 "And when I broke the seven loaves for the
four thousand people," asked Jesus, "how many baskets full of leftover pieces did you take up?"

"Seven," they answered.

21 "And you still don't understand?" he asked them.

Jesus Heals a Blind Man at Bethsaida

22 They came to Bethsaida, where some people
brought a blind man to Jesus and begged him to
touch him. ²³Jesus took the blind man by the hand
and led him out of the village. After spitting on the
man's eyes, Jesus placed his hands on him and asked
him, "Can you see anything?"

24 The man looked up and said, "Yes, I can see
people, but they look like trees walking about."

25 Jesus again placed his hands on the man's eyes.
This time the man looked intently, his eyesight
returned, and he saw everything clearly. ²⁶Jesus then
sent him home with the order, "Don't go back into
the village."

Peter's Declaration about Jesus
(Matt. 16.13–20; Luke 9.18–21)

27 Then Jesus and his disciples went away to the
villages near Caesarea Philippi. On the way he asked

He must forget self, carry his cross, and follow me (8.34)

them, "Tell me, who do people say I am?"

28 "Some say that you are John the Baptist," they answered; "others say that you are Elijah, while others say that you are one of the prophets."

29 "What about you?" he asked them. "Who do you say I am?"

Peter answered, "You are the Messiah."

30 Then Jesus ordered them, "Do not tell anyone about me."

Jesus Speaks about His Suffering and Death
(Matt. 16.21-28; Luke 9.22-27)

31 Then Jesus began to teach his disciples: "The Son of Man must suffer much and be rejected by the elders, the chief priests, and the teachers of the Law. He will be put to death, but three days later he will rise to life." 32 He made this very clear to them. So Peter took him aside and began to rebuke him. 33 But Jesus turned round, looked at his disciples, and rebuked Peter. "Get away from me, Satan," he said. "Your thoughts don't come from God but from man!"

34 Then Jesus called the crowd and his disciples to him. "If anyone wants to come with me," he told them, "he must forget self, carry his cross, and follow me. 35 For whoever wants to save his own life will lose it; but whoever loses his life for me and for the gospel will save it. 36 Does a person gain anything if he wins the whole world but loses his life? Of course not! 37 There is nothing he can give to regain

his life. ³⁸If a person is ashamed of me and of my teaching in this godless and wicked day, then the Son of Man will be ashamed of him when he comes in the glory of his Father with the holy angels."

9 And he went on to say, "I tell you, there are some here who will not die until they have seen the Kingdom of God come with power."

The Transfiguration
(Matt. 17.1–13; Luke 9.28–36)

2 Six days later Jesus took with him Peter, James, and John, and led them up a high mountain, where they were alone. As they looked on, a change came over Jesus, ³and his clothes became shining white—whiter than anyone in the world could wash them. ⁴Then the three disciples saw Elijah and Moses talking with Jesus. ⁵Peter spoke up and said to Jesus, "Teacher, how good it is that we are here! We will make three tents, one for you, one for Moses, and one for Elijah." ⁶He and the others were so frightened that he did not know what to say.

7 Then a cloud appeared and covered them with its shadow, and a voice came from the cloud, "This is my own dear Son—listen to him!" ⁸They took a quick look round but did not see anyone else; only Jesus was with them.

9 As they came down the mountain, Jesus ordered them, "Don't tell anyone what you have seen, until the Son of Man has risen from death."

10 They obeyed his order, but among themselves they started discussing the matter, "What does this 'rising from death' mean?" ¹¹And they asked Jesus, "Why do the teachers of the Law say that Elijah has to come first?"

12 His answer was, "Elijah is indeed coming first in order to get everything ready. Yet why do the Scriptures say that the Son of Man will suffer much and be rejected? ¹³I tell you, however, that Elijah has already come and that people treated him just as they pleased, as the Scriptures say about him."

Jesus Heals a Boy with an Evil Spirit
(Matt. 17.14–21; Luke 9.37–43a)

14 When they joined the rest of the disciples, they saw a large crowd round them and some teachers of the Law arguing with them. 15 When the people saw Jesus, they were greatly surprised, and ran to him and greeted him. 16 Jesus asked his disciples, "What are you arguing with them about?"

17 A man in the crowd answered, "Teacher, I brought my son to you, because he has an evil spirit in him and cannot talk. 18 Whenever the spirit attacks him, it throws him to the ground, and he foams at the mouth, grits his teeth, and becomes stiff all over. I asked your disciples to drive the spirit out, but they could not."

19 Jesus said to them, "How unbelieving you people are! How long must I stay with you? How long do I have to put up with you? Bring the boy to me!" 20 They brought him to Jesus.

As soon as the spirit saw Jesus, it threw the boy into a fit, so that he fell on the ground and rolled round, foaming at the mouth. 21 "How long has he been like this?" Jesus asked the father.

"Ever since he was a child," he replied. 22 "Many times the evil spirit has tried to kill him by throwing him in the fire and into water. Have pity on us and help us, if you possibly can!"

23 "Yes," said Jesus, "if you yourself can! Everything is possible for the person who has faith."

24 The father at once cried out, "I do have faith, but not enough. Help me to have more!"

25 Jesus noticed that the crowd was closing in on them, so he gave a command to the evil spirit. "Deaf and dumb spirit," he said, "I order you to come out of the boy and never go into him again!"

26 The spirit screamed, threw the boy into a bad fit, and came out. The boy looked like a corpse, and everyone said, "He is dead!" 27 But Jesus took the boy by the hand and helped him to rise, and he stood up.

28 After Jesus had gone indoors, his disciples asked him privately, "Why couldn't we drive the spirit out?"

29 "Only prayer can drive this kind out," answered Jesus; "nothing else can."

Jesus Speaks Again about His Death
(Matt. 17.22–23; Luke 9.43b–45)

30 Jesus and his disciples left that place and went on through Galilee. Jesus did not want anyone to know where he was, 31 because he was teaching his disciples: "The Son of Man will be handed over to men who will kill him. Three days later, however, he will rise to life."

32 But they did not understand what this teaching meant, and they were afraid to ask him.

Who Is the Greatest?
(Matt. 18.1–5; Luke 9.46–48)

33 They came to Capernaum, and after going indoors Jesus asked his disciples, "What were you arguing about on the road?"

34 But they would not answer him, because on the road they had been arguing among themselves about who was the greatest. 35 Jesus sat down, called the twelve disciples, and said to them, "Whoever wants to be first must place himself last of all and be the servant of all." 36 Then he took a child and made him stand in front of them. He put his arms round him and said to them, 37 "Whoever welcomes in my name one of these children, welcomes me; and whoever welcomes me, welcomes not only me but also the one who sent me."

Whoever Is Not against Us Is for Us
(Luke 9.49–50)

38 John said to him, "Teacher, we saw a man who was driving out demons in your name, and we told him to stop, because he doesn't belong to our group."

39 "Do not try to stop him," Jesus told them, "because no one who performs a miracle in my name will be able soon afterwards to say evil things about me. 40 For whoever is not against us is for us. 41 I assure you that anyone who gives you a drink of water because you belong to me will certainly receive his reward.

Temptations to Sin
(Matt. 18.6-9; Luke 17.1-2)

42 "If anyone should cause one of these little ones
to lose his faith in me, it would be better for that
person to have a large millstone tied round his neck
and be thrown into the sea. 43 So if your hand makes
you lose your faith, cut it off! It is better for you
to enter life without a hand than to keep both hands
and go off to hell, to the fire that never goes out. *o*
45 And if your foot makes you lose your faith, cut
it off! It is better for you to enter life without a
foot than to keep both feet and be thrown into hell. *p*
47 And if your eye makes you lose your faith, take
it out! It is better for you to enter the Kingdom
of God with only one eye than to keep both eyes
and be thrown into hell. 48 There 'the worms that
eat them never die, and the fire that burns them
is never put out.'

49 "Everyone will be purified by fire as a sacrifice
is purified by salt.

50 "Salt is good; but if it loses its saltiness, how
can you make it salty again?

"Have the salt of friendship among yourselves, and
live in peace with one another."

Jesus Teaches about Divorce
(Matt. 19.1-12; Luke 16.18)

10 Then Jesus left that place, went to the province
of Judaea, and crossed the River Jordan. Crowds
came flocking to him again, and he taught them, as
he always did.

2 Some Pharisees came to him and tried to trap
him. "Tell us," they asked, "does our Law allow a
man to divorce his wife?"

o Some manuscripts add verse 44: There 'the worms that eat
them never die, and the fire that burns them is never put out'
(see verse 48).
p Some manuscripts add verse 46: There 'the worms that eat
them never die, and the fire that burns them is never put out'
(see verse 48).

3 Jesus answered with a question, "What law did Moses give you?"

4 Their answer was, "Moses gave permission for a man to write a divorce notice and send his wife away."

5 Jesus said to them, "Moses wrote this law for you because you are so hard to teach. 6 But in the beginning, at the time of creation, 'God made them male and female,' as the scripture says. 7 'And for this reason a man will leave his father and mother and unite with his wife,*q* 8 and the two will become one.' So they are no longer two, but one. 9 Man must not separate, then, what God has joined together."

10 When they went back into the house, the disciples asked Jesus about this matter. 11 He said to them, "A man who divorces his wife and marries another woman commits adultery against his wife. 12 In the same way, a woman who divorces her husband and marries another man commits adultery."

Jesus Blesses Little Children
(Matt. 19.13–15; Luke 18.15–17)

13 Some people brought children to Jesus for him to place his hands on them, but the disciples scolded the people. 14 When Jesus noticed this, he was angry and said to his disciples, "Let the children come to me, and do not stop them, because the Kingdom of God belongs to such as these. 15 I assure you that whoever does not receive the Kingdom of God like a child will never enter it." 16 Then he took the children in his arms, placed his hands on each of them, and blessed them.

The Rich Man
(Matt. 19.16–30; Luke 18.18–30)

17 As Jesus was starting on his way again, a man ran up, knelt before him, and asked him, "Good Teacher, what must I do to receive eternal life?"

18 "Why do you call me good?" Jesus asked him. "No one is good except God alone. 19 You know the commandments: 'Do not commit murder; do not com-

q Some manuscripts do not have and unite with his wife.

mit adultery; do not steal; do not accuse anyone falsely; do not cheat; respect your father and your mother.' "

20 "Teacher," the man said, "ever since I was young, I have obeyed all these commandments."

21 Jesus looked straight at him with love and said, "You need only one thing. Go and sell all you have and give the money to the poor, and you will have riches in heaven; then come and follow me." 22 When the man heard this, gloom spread over his face, and he went away sad, because he was very rich.

23 Jesus looked round at his disciples and said to them, "How hard it will be for rich people to enter the Kingdom of God!"

24 The disciples were shocked at these words, but Jesus went on to say, "My children, how hard it is to enter the Kingdom of God! 25 It is much harder for a rich person to enter the Kingdom of God than for a camel to go through the eye of a needle."

26 At this the disciples were completely amazed and asked one another, "Who, then, can be saved?"

27 Jesus looked straight at them and answered, "This is impossible for man, but not for God; everything is possible for God."

28 Then Peter spoke up, "Look, we have left everything and followed you."

29 "Yes," Jesus said to them, "and I tell you that anyone who leaves home or brothers or sisters or mother or father or children or fields for me and for the gospel, 30 will receive much more in this present age. He will receive a hundred times more houses, brothers, sisters, mothers, children and fields—and persecutions as well; and in the age to come he will receive eternal life. 31 But many who now are first will be last, and many who now are last will be first."

Jesus Speaks a Third Time about His Death
(Matt. 20.17-19; Luke 18.31-34)

32 Jesus and his disciples were now on the road going up to Jerusalem. Jesus was going ahead of the disciples, who were filled with alarm; the people who followed behind were afraid. Once again Jesus

took the twelve disciples aside and spoke of the things
that were going to happen to him. 33"Listen," he
told them, "we are going up to Jerusalem where the
Son of Man will be handed over to the chief priests
and the teachers of the Law. They will condemn him
to death and then hand him over to the Gentiles,
34who will mock him, spit on him, whip him, and
kill him; but three days later he will rise to life."

The Request of James and John
(Matt. 20.20–28)

35 Then James and John, the sons of Zebedee, came
to Jesus. "Teacher," they said, "there is something
we want you to do for us."

36 "What is it?" Jesus asked them.

37 They answered, "When you sit on your throne
in your glorious Kingdom, we want you to let us
sit with you, one at your right and one at your left."

38 Jesus said to them, "You don't know what you
are asking for. Can you drink the cup of suffering
that I must drink? Can you be baptized in the way
I must be baptized?"

39 "We can," they answered.

Jesus said to them, "You will indeed drink the cup
I must drink and be baptized in the way I must
be baptized. 40But I do not have the right to choose
who will sit at my right and my left. It is God who
will give these places to those for whom he has prepared them."

41 When the other ten disciples heard about it, they
became angry with James and John. 42So Jesus called
them all together to him and said, "You know that
the men who are considered rulers of the heathen have
power over them, and the leaders have complete
authority. 43This, however, is not the way it is among
you. If one of you wants to be great, he must be
the servant of the rest; 44and if one of you wants
to be first, he must be the slave of all. 45For even
the Son of Man did not come to be served; he came
to serve and to give his life to redeem many people."

Jesus Heals Blind Bartimaeus
(Matt. 20.29–34; Luke 18.35–43)

46 They came to Jericho, and as Jesus was leaving with his disciples and a large crowd, a blind beggar named Bartimaeus son of Timaeus was sitting by the road. ⁴⁷When he heard that it was Jesus of Nazareth, he began to shout, "Jesus! Son of David! Take pity on me!"

48 Many of the people scolded him and told him to be quiet. But he shouted even more loudly, "Son of David, take pity on me!"

49 Jesus stopped and said, "Call him."

So they called the blind man. "Cheer up!" they said. "Get up, he is calling you."

50 He threw off his cloak, jumped up, and came to Jesus.

51 "What do you want me to do for you?" Jesus asked him.

"Teacher," the blind man answered, "I want to see again."

52 "Go," Jesus told him, "your faith has made you well."

At once he was able to see and followed Jesus on the road.

The Triumphant Entry into Jerusalem
(Matt. 21.1–11; Luke 19.28–40; John 12.12–19)

11 As they approached Jerusalem, near the towns of Bethphage and Bethany, they came to the Mount of Olives. Jesus sent two of his disciples on ahead ²with these instructions: "Go to the village there ahead of you. As soon as you get there, you will find a colt tied up that has never been ridden. Untie it and bring it here. ³And if someone asks you why you are doing that, tell him that the Master ʳ needs it and will send it back at once."

4 So they went and found a colt out in the street, tied to the door of a house. As they were untying it, ⁵some of the bystanders asked them, "What are you doing, untying that colt?"

ʳthe Master; *or* its owner.

6 They answered just as Jesus had told them, and the men let them go. ⁷They brought the colt to Jesus, threw their cloaks over the animal, and Jesus got on. ⁸Many people spread their cloaks on the road, while others cut branches in the fields and spread them on the road. ⁹The people who were in front and those who followed behind began to shout, "Praise God! God bless him who comes in the name of the Lord! ¹⁰God bless the coming kingdom of King David, our father! Praise God!"

11 Jesus entered Jerusalem, went into the Temple, and looked round at everything. But since it was already late in the day, he went out to Bethany with the twelve disciples.

Jesus Curses the Fig-Tree
(Matt. 21.18–19)

12 The next day, as they were coming back from Bethany, Jesus was hungry. ¹³He saw in the distance a fig-tree covered with leaves, so he went to see if he could find any figs on it. But when he came to it, he found only leaves, because it was not the right time for figs. ¹⁴Jesus said to the fig-tree, "No one shall ever eat figs from you again!"

And his disciples heard him.

Jesus Goes to the Temple
(Matt. 21.12–17; Luke 19.45–48; John 2.13–22)

15 When they arrived in Jerusalem, Jesus went to the Temple and began to drive out all those who were buying and selling. He overturned the tables of the money-changers and the stools of those who sold pigeons, ¹⁶and he would not let anyone carry anything through the temple courtyards. ¹⁷He then taught the people: "It is written in the Scriptures that God said, 'My Temple will be called a house of prayer for the people of all nations.' But you have turned it into a hideout for thieves!"

18 The chief priests and the teachers of the Law heard of this, so they began looking for some way to kill Jesus. They were afraid of him, because the whole crowd was amazed at his teaching.

19 When evening came, Jesus and his disciples left the city.

The Lesson from the Fig-Tree
(Matt. 21.20–22)

20 Early next morning, as they walked along the road, they saw the fig-tree. It was dead all the way down to its roots. 21 Peter remembered what had happened and said to Jesus, "Look, Teacher, the fig-tree you cursed has died!"

22 Jesus answered them, "Have faith in God. 23 I assure you that whoever tells this hill to get up and throw itself in the sea and does not doubt in his heart, but believes that what he says will happen, it will be done for him. 24 For this reason I tell you: When you pray and ask for something, believe that you have received it, and you will be given whatever you ask for. 25 And when you stand and pray, forgive anything you may have against anyone, so that your Father in heaven will forgive the wrongs you have done." *s*

The Question about Jesus' Authority
(Matt. 21.23–27; Luke 20.1–8)

27 They arrived once again in Jerusalem. As Jesus was walking in the Temple, the chief priests, the teachers of the Law, and the elders came to him 28 and asked him, "What right have you to do these things? Who gave you this right?"

29 Jesus answered them, "I will ask you just one question, and if you give me an answer, I will tell you what right I have to do these things. 30 Tell me, where did John's right to baptize come from: was it from God or from man?"

31 They started to argue among themselves: "What shall we say? If we answer, 'From God,' he will say, 'Why, then, did you not believe John?' 32 But if we say, 'From man . . .'" (They were afraid of the people, because everyone was convinced that John

s Some manuscripts add verse 26: If you do not forgive others, your Father in heaven will not forgive the wrongs you have done *(see Mt 6.15).*

had been a prophet.) ³³So their answer to Jesus was, "We don't know."

Jesus said to them, "Neither will I tell you, then, by what right I do these things."

The Parable of the Tenants in the Vineyard
(Matt. 21.33-46; Luke 20.9-19)

12 Then Jesus spoke to them in parables: "Once there was a man who planted a vineyard, put a fence round it, dug a hole for the winepress, and built a watch-tower. Then he let out the vineyard to tenants and left home on a journey. ²When the time came to gather the grapes, he sent a slave to the tenants to receive from them his share of the harvest. ³The tenants seized the slave, beat him, and sent him back without a thing. ⁴Then the owner sent another slave; the tenants beat him over the head and treated him shamefully. ⁵The owner sent another slave, and they killed him; and they treated many others the same way, beating some and killing others. ⁶The only one left to send was the man's own dear son. Last of all, then, he sent his son to the tenants. 'I am sure they will respect my son,' he said. ⁷But those tenants said to one another, 'This is the owner's son. Come on, let's kill him, and his property will be ours!' ⁸So they seized the son and killed him and threw his body out of the vineyard.

9 "What, then, will the owner of the vineyard do?" asked Jesus. "He will come and kill those men and hand the vineyard over to other tenants. ¹⁰Surely you have read this scripture?

'The stone which the builders rejected as worthless
turned out to be the most important of all.

¹¹ This was done by the Lord;
what a wonderful sight it is!' "

12 The Jewish leaders tried to arrest Jesus, because they knew that he had told this parable against them. But they were afraid of the crowd, so they left him and went away.

The Question about Paying Taxes
(Matt. 22.15-22; Luke 20.20-26)

13 Some Pharisees and some members of Herod's

party were sent to Jesus to trap him with questions.
14They came to him and said, "Teacher, we know
that you tell the truth, without worrying about what
people think. You pay no attention to a man's status,
but teach the truth about God's will for man. Tell
us, is it against our Law to pay taxes to the Roman
Emperor? Should we pay them or not?"

15 But Jesus saw through their trick and answered,
"Why are you trying to trap me? Bring a silver coin,
and let me see it."

16 They brought him one, and he asked, "Whose
face and name are these?"

"The Emperor's," they answered.

17 So Jesus said, "Well, then, pay the Emperor what
belongs to the Emperor, and pay God what belongs
to God."

And they were amazed at Jesus.

The Question about Rising from Death
(Matt. 22.23–33; Luke 20.27–40)

18 Then some Sadducees, who say that people will
not rise from death, came to Jesus and said,
19"Teacher, Moses wrote this law for us: 'If a man
dies and leaves a wife but no children, that man's
brother must marry the widow so that they can have
children who will be considered the dead man's children.' 20Once there were seven brothers; the eldest got
married and died without having children. 21Then the
second one married the woman, and he also died
without having children. The same thing happened
to the third brother, 22and then to the rest: all seven
brothers married the woman and died without having
children. Last of all, the woman died. 23Now, when
all the dead rise to life on the day of resurrection,
whose wife will she be? All seven of them had married
her."

24 Jesus answered them, "How wrong you are! And
do you know why? It is because you don't know
the Scriptures or God's power. 25For when the dead
rise to life, they will be like the angels in heaven
and will not marry. 26Now, as for the dead being
raised: haven't you ever read in the Book of Moses
the passage about the burning bush? There it is written

that God said to Moses, 'I am the God of Abraham, the God of Isaac, and the God of Jacob.' [27]He is the God of the living, not of the dead. You are completely wrong!"

The Great Commandment
(Matt. 22.34–40; Luke 10.25–28)

28 A teacher of the Law was there who heard the discussion. He saw that Jesus had given the Sadducees a good answer, so he came to him with a question: "Which commandment is the most important of all?"

29 Jesus replied, "The most important one is this: 'Listen, Israel! The Lord our God is the only Lord.[t] [30]Love the Lord your God with all your heart, with all your soul, with all your mind, and with all your strength.' [31]The second most important commandment is this: 'Love your neighbour as you love yourself.' There is no other commandment more important than these two."

32 The teacher of the Law said to Jesus, "Well done, Teacher! It is true, as you say, that only the Lord is God and that there is no other god but he. [33]And man must love God with all his heart and with all his mind and with all his strength; and he must love his neighbour as he loves himself. It is more important to obey these two commandments than to offer animals and other sacrifices to God."

34 Jesus noticed how wise his answer was, and so he told him, "You are not far from the Kingdom of God."

After this nobody dared to ask Jesus any more questions.

The Question about the Messiah
(Matt. 22.41–46; Luke 20.41–44)

35 As Jesus was teaching in the Temple, he asked the question, "How can the teachers of the Law say that the Messiah will be the descendant of David? [36]The Holy Spirit inspired David to say:

'The Lord said to my Lord:

[t]The Lord our God is the only Lord; or The Lord is our God, the Lord alone.

    Sit here on my right
    until I put your enemies under your feet.'
37 David himself called him 'Lord'; so how can the Messiah be David's descendant?"

Jesus Warns against the Teachers of the Law
(Matt. 23.1–36; Luke 20.45–47)

A large crowd was listening to Jesus gladly. 38 As he taught them, he said, "Watch out for the teachers of the Law, who like to walk around in their long robes and be greeted with respect in the market-place, 39 who choose the reserved seats in the synagogues and the best places at feasts. 40 They take advantage of widows and rob them of their homes, and then make a show of saying long prayers. Their punishment will be all the worse!"

The Widow's Offering
(Luke 21.1–4)

41 As Jesus sat near the temple treasury, he watched the people as they dropped in their money. Many rich men dropped in a lot of money; 42 then a poor widow came along and dropped in two little copper

A poor widow came along (12.42)

coins, worth about a penny. 43 He called his disciples together and said to them, "I tell you that this poor widow put more in the offering box than all the others. 44 For the others put in what they had to spare of their riches; but she, poor as she is, put in all she had—she gave all she had to live on."

Jesus Speaks of the Destruction of the Temple
(Matt. 24.1-2; Luke 21.5-6)

13 As Jesus was leaving the Temple, one of his disciples said, "Look, Teacher! What wonderful stones and buildings!"

2 Jesus answered, "You see these great buildings? Not a single stone here will be left in its place; every one of them will be thrown down."

Troubles and Persecutions
(Matt. 24.3-14; Luke 21.7-19)

3 Jesus was sitting on the Mount of Olives, across from the Temple, when Peter, James, John, and Andrew came to him in private. 4 "Tell us when this will be," they said, "and tell us what will happen to show that the time has come for all these things to take place."

5 Jesus said to them, "Be on guard, and don't let anyone deceive you. 6 Many men, claiming to speak for me, will come and say, 'I am he!' and they will deceive many people. 7 And don't be troubled when you hear the noise of battles close by and news of battles far away. Such things must happen, but they do not mean that the end has come. 8 Countries will fight each other; kingdoms will attack one another. There will be earthquakes everywhere, and there will be famines. These things are like the first pains of child-birth.

9 "You yourselves must be on guard. You will be arrested and taken to court. You will be beaten in the synagogues; you will stand before rulers and kings for my sake to tell them the Good News. 10 But before the end comes, the gospel must be preached to all peoples. 11 And when you are arrested and taken to court, do not worry beforehand about what you are going to say; when the time comes, say whatever

is then given to you. For the words you speak will not be yours; they will come from the Holy Spirit. 12 Men will hand over their own brothers to be put to death, and fathers will do the same to their children. Children will turn against their parents and have them put to death. 13 Everyone will hate you because of me. But whoever holds out to the end will be saved.

The Awful Horror
(Matt. 24.15–28; Luke 21.20–24)

14 "You will see 'The Awful Horror' standing in the place where he should not be." (Note to the reader: be sure to understand what this means!) "Then those who are in Judaea must run away to the hills. 15 A man who is on the roof of his house must not lose time by going down into the house to get anything to take with him. 16 A man who is in the field must not go back to the house for his cloak. 17 How terrible it will be in those days for women who are pregnant and for mothers with little babies! 18 Pray to God that these things will not happen in the winter! 19 For the trouble of those days will be far worse than any the world has ever known from the very beginning when God created the world until the present time. Nor will there ever be anything like it again. 20 But the Lord has reduced the number of those days; if he had not, nobody would survive. For the sake of his chosen people, however, he has reduced those days.

21 "Then, if anyone says to you, 'Look, here is the Messiah!' or, 'Look, there he is!'—do not believe him. 22 For false Messiahs and false prophets will appear. They will perform miracles and wonders in order to deceive even God's chosen people, if possible. 23 Be on your guard! I have told you everything before the time comes.

The Coming of the Son of Man
(Matt. 24.29–31; Luke 21.25–28)

24 "In the days after that time of trouble the sun will grow dark, the moon will no longer shine, 25 the stars will fall from heaven, and the powers in space will be driven from their courses. 26 Then the Son of

Man will appear, coming in the clouds with great power and glory. 27 He will send the angels out to the four corners of the earth to gather God's chosen people from one end of the world to the other.

The Lesson of the Fig-Tree
(Matt. 24.32–35; Luke 21.29–33)

28 "Let the fig-tree teach you a lesson. When its branches become green and tender and it starts putting out leaves, you know that summer is near. 29 In the same way, when you see these things happening, you will know that the time is near, ready to begin.ᵘ 30 Remember that all these things will happen before the people now living have all died. 31 Heaven and earth will pass away, but my words will never pass away.

No One Knows the Day or Hour
(Matt. 24.36–44)

32 "No one knows, however, when that day or hour will come—neither the angels in heaven, nor the Son; only the Father knows. 33 Be on watch, be alert, for you do not know when the time will come. 34 It will be like a man who goes away from home on a journey and leaves his servants in charge, after giving to each one his own work to do and after telling the doorkeeper to keep watch. 35 Be on guard, then, because you do not know when the master of the house is coming—it might be in the evening or at midnight or before dawn or at sunrise. 36 If he comes suddenly, he must not find you asleep. 37 What I say to you, then, I say to all: Watch!"

The Plot against Jesus
(Matt. 26.1–5; Luke 22.1–2; John 11.45–53)

14 It was now two days before the Festival of Passover and Unleavened Bread. The chief priests and the teachers of the Law were looking for a way to arrest Jesus secretly and put him to death. 2 "We must not do it during the festival," they said, "or the people might riot."

ᵘthe time is near, ready to begin; or he is near, ready to come.

Jesus Is Anointed at Bethany
(Matt. 26.6–13; John 12.1–8)

3 Jesus was in Bethany at the house of Simon, a man who had suffered from a dreaded skin-disease. While Jesus was eating, a woman came in with an alabaster jar full of a very expensive perfume made of pure nard. She broke the jar and poured the perfume on Jesus' head. ⁴Some of the people there became angry and said to one another, "What was the use of wasting the perfume? ⁵It could have been sold for more than three hundred silver coins*ᵛ* and the money given to the poor!" And they criticized her harshly.
6 But Jesus said, "Leave her alone! Why are you bothering her? She has done a fine and beautiful thing for me. ⁷You will always have poor people with you, and any time you want to, you can help them. But you will not always have me. ⁸She did what she could; she poured perfume on my body to prepare it ahead of time for burial. ⁹Now, I assure you that wherever the gospel is preached all over the world, what she has done will be told in memory of her."

Judas Agrees to Betray Jesus
(Matt. 26.14–16; Luke 22.3–6)

10 Then Judas Iscariot, one of the twelve disciples, went off to the chief priests in order to betray Jesus to them. ¹¹They were pleased to hear what he had to say, and promised to give him money. So Judas started looking for a good chance to hand Jesus over to them.

Jesus Eats the Passover Meal with His Disciples
(Matt. 26.17–25; Luke 22.7–14, 21–23; John 13.21–30)

12 On the first day of the Festival of Unleavened Bread, the day the lambs for the Passover meal were killed, Jesus' disciples asked him, "Where do you want us to go and get the Passover meal ready for you?"
13 Then Jesus sent two of them with these instructions: "Go into the city, and a man carrying a jar

*ᵛ*SILVER COINS: *See 6.37.*

of water will meet you. Follow him [14]to the house he enters, and say to the owner of the house: 'The Teacher says, Where is the room where my disciples and I will eat the Passover meal?' [15]Then he will show you a large upstairs room, prepared and furnished, where you will get everything ready for us."

16 The disciples left, went to the city, and found everything just as Jesus had told them; and they prepared the Passover meal.

17 When it was evening, Jesus came with the twelve disciples. [18]While they were at the table eating, Jesus said, "I tell you that one of you will betray me—one who is eating with me."

19 The disciples were upset and began to ask him, one after the other, "Surely you don't mean me, do you?"

20 Jesus answered, "It will be one of you twelve, one who dips his bread in the dish with me. [21]The Son of Man will die as the Scriptures say he will; but how terrible for that man who betrays the Son of Man! It would have been better for that man if he had never been born!"

The Lord's Supper
(Matt. 26.26–30; Luke 22.14–20; I Cor. 11.23–25)

22 While they were eating, Jesus took a piece of bread, gave a prayer of thanks, broke it, and gave

This is my body (14.22)

it to his disciples. "Take it," he said, "this is my body."

23 Then he took a cup, gave thanks to God, and handed it to them; and they all drank from it. 24 Jesus said, "This is my blood which is poured out for many, my blood which seals God's covenant. 25 I tell you, I will never again drink this wine until the day I drink the new wine in the Kingdom of God."

26 Then they sang a hymn and went out to the Mount of Olives.

Jesus Predicts Peter's Denial
(Matt. 26.31–35; Luke 22.31–34; John 13.36–38)

27 Jesus said to them, "All of you will run away and leave me, for the scripture says, 'God will kill the shepherd, and the sheep will all be scattered.' 28 But after I am raised to life, I will go to Galilee ahead of you."

29 Peter answered, "I will never leave you, even though all the rest do!"

30 Jesus said to Peter, "I tell you that before the cock crows twice tonight, you will say three times that you do not know me."

31 Peter answered even more strongly, "I will never say that, even if I have to die with you!"

And all the other disciples said the same thing.

Jesus Prays in Gethsemane
(Matt. 26.36–46; Luke 22.39–46)

32 They came to a place called Gethsemane, and Jesus said to his disciples, "Sit here while I pray." 33 He took Peter, James, and John with him. Distress and anguish came over him, 34 and he said to them, "The sorrow in my heart is so great that it almost crushes me. Stay here and keep watch."

35 He went a little farther on, threw himself on the ground, and prayed that, if possible, he might not have to go through that time of suffering. 36 "Father," he prayed, "my Father! All things are possible for you. Take this cup of suffering away from me. Yet not what I want, but what you want."

37 Then he returned and found the three disciples asleep. He said to Peter, "Simon, are you asleep?

Weren't you able to stay awake even for one hour?"
³⁸ And he said to them, "Keep watch, and pray that you
will not fall into temptation. The spirit is willing,
but the flesh is weak."

39 He went away once more and prayed, saying
the same words. ⁴⁰ Then he came back to the disciples
and found them asleep; they could not keep their
eyes open. And they did not know what to say to
him.

41 When he came back the third time, he said to
them, "Are you still sleeping and resting? Enough!
The hour has come! Look, the Son of Man is now
being handed over to the power of sinful men. ⁴² Get
up, let us go. Look, here is the man who is betraying
me!"

The Arrest of Jesus
(Matt. 26.47-56; Luke 22.47-53; John 18.3-12)

43 Jesus was still speaking when Judas, one of the
twelve disciples, arrived. With him was a crowd armed
with swords and clubs, and sent by the chief priests,
the teachers of the Law, and the elders. ⁴⁴ The traitor
had given the crowd a signal: "The man I kiss is
the one you want. Arrest him and take him away
under guard."

45 As soon as Judas arrived, he went up to Jesus
and said, "Teacher!" and kissed him. ⁴⁶ So they arrested
Jesus and held him tight. ⁴⁷ But one of those standing
there drew his sword and struck at the High Priest's
slave, cutting off his ear. ⁴⁸ Then Jesus spoke up and
said to them, "Did you have to come with swords
and clubs to capture me, as though I were an outlaw?
⁴⁹ Day after day I was with you teaching in the Temple,
and you did not arrest me. But the Scriptures must
come true."

50 Then all the disciples left him and ran away.

51 A certain young man, dressed only in a linen
cloth, was following Jesus. They tried to arrest him,
⁵² but he ran away naked, leaving the cloth behind.

Jesus before the Council
(Matt. 26.57-68; Luke 22.54-55, 63-71; John 18.13-14, 19-24)

53 Then Jesus was taken to the High Priest's house,

So they arrested Jesus and held him tight (14.46)

where all the chief priests, the elders, and the teachers of the Law were gathering. ⁵⁴Peter followed from a distance and went into the courtyard of the High Priest's house. There he sat down with the guards, keeping himself warm by the fire. ⁵⁵The chief priests and the whole Council tried to find some evidence against Jesus in order to put him to death, but they could not find any. ⁵⁶Many witnesses told lies against Jesus, but their stories did not agree.

57 Then some men stood up and told this lie against Jesus: ⁵⁸"We heard him say, 'I will tear down this Temple which men have made, and after three days I will build one that is not made by men.' " ⁵⁹Not even they, however, could make their stories agree.

60 The High Priest stood up in front of them all and questioned Jesus, "Have you no answer to the accusation they bring against you?"

61 But Jesus kept quiet and would not say a word. Again the High Priest questioned him, "Are you the Messiah, the Son of the Blessed God?"

62 "I am," answered Jesus, "and you will all see

the Son of Man seated on the right of the Almighty
and coming with the clouds of heaven!"

63 The High Priest tore his robes and said, "We
don't need any more witnesses! 64 You heard his blasphemy. What is your decision?"

They all voted against him: he was guilty and should
be put to death.

65 Some of them began to spit on Jesus, and they
blindfolded him and hit him. "Guess who hit you!"
they said. And the guards took him and slapped him.

Peter Denies Jesus
(Matt. 26.69–75; Luke 22.56–62; John 18.15–18, 25–27)

66 Peter was still down in the courtyard when one
of the High Priest's servant-girls came by. 67 When
she saw Peter warming himself, she looked straight
at him and said, "You, too, were with Jesus of
Nazareth."

68 But he denied it. "I don't know... I don't understand what you are talking about," he answered, and
went out into the passage. Just then a cock crowed. w

69 The servant-girl saw him there and began to
repeat to the bystanders, "He is one of them!" 70 But
Peter denied it again.

A little while later the bystanders accused Peter
again, "You can't deny that you are one of them,
because you, too, are from Galilee."

71 Then Peter said, "I swear that I am telling the
truth! May God punish me if I am not! I do not
know the man you are talking about!"

72 Just then a cock crowed a second time, and
Peter remembered how Jesus had said to him, "Before
the cock crows twice, you will say three times that
you do not know me." And he broke down and cried.

Jesus Is Brought before Pilate
(Matt. 27.1–2, 11–14; Luke 23.1–5; John 18.28–38)

15 Early in the morning the chief priests met hur-
riedly with the elders, the teachers of the Law,
and the whole Council, and made their plans. They
put Jesus in chains, led him away, and handed him

---

w Some manuscripts do not have Just then a cock crowed.

A cock crowed...and Peter remembered (14.72)

over to Pilate. ²Pilate questioned him, "Are you the
king of the Jews?"

Jesus answered, "So you say."

3 The chief priests were accusing Jesus of many
things, ⁴so Pilate questioned him again, "Aren't you
going to answer? Listen to all their accusations!"

5 Again Jesus refused to say a word, and Pilate
was amazed.

Jesus Is Sentenced to Death
(Matt. 27.15-26; Luke 23.13-25; John 18.39—19.16)

6 At every Passover Festival Pilate was in the habit
of setting free any one prisoner the people asked
for. ⁷At that time a man named Barabbas was in
prison with the rebels who had committed murder
in the riot. ⁸When the crowd gathered and began
to ask Pilate for the usual favour, ⁹he asked them,
"Do you want me to set free for you the king of
the Jews?" ¹⁰He knew very well that the chief priests
had handed Jesus over to him because they were
jealous.

11 But the chief priests stirred up the crowd to
ask, instead, for Pilate to set Barabbas free for them.

¹²Pilate spoke again to the crowd, "What, then, do you want me to do with the one you call the king of the Jews?"

13 They shouted back, "Crucify him!"

14 "But what crime has he committed?" Pilate asked. They shouted all the louder, "Crucify him!"

15 Pilate wanted to please the crowd, so he set Barabbas free for them. Then he had Jesus whipped and handed him over to be crucified.

The Soldiers Mock Jesus
(Matt. 27.27–31; John 19.2–3)

16 The soldiers took Jesus inside to the courtyard of the governor's palace and called together the rest of the company. ¹⁷They put a purple robe on Jesus, made a crown out of thorny branches, and put it on his head. ¹⁸Then they began to salute him: "Long live the King of the Jews!" ¹⁹They beat him over the head with a stick, spat on him, fell on their knees, and bowed down to him. ²⁰When they had finished mocking him, they took off the purple robe and put his own clothes back on him. Then they led him out to crucify him.

Jesus Is Crucified
(Matt. 27.32–44; Luke 23.26–43; John 19.17–27)

21 On the way they met a man named Simon, who was coming into the city from the country, and the soldiers forced him to carry Jesus' cross. (Simon was from Cyrene and was the father of Alexander and Rufus.) ²²They took Jesus to a place called Golgotha, which means "The Place of the Skull." ²³There they tried to give him wine mixed with a drug called myrrh, but Jesus would not drink it. ²⁴Then they crucified him and divided his clothes among themselves, throwing dice to see who would get which piece of clothing. ²⁵It was nine o'clock in the morning when they crucified him. ²⁶The notice of the accusation against him said: "The King of the Jews." ²⁷They also crucified

two bandits with Jesus, one on his right and the other on his left.ˣ

29 People passing by shook their heads and hurled insults at Jesus: "Aha! You were going to tear down the Temple and build it up again in three days! ³⁰ Now come down from the cross and save yourself!"

Throwing dice (15.24)

31 In the same way the chief priests and the teachers of the Law jeered at Jesus, saying to each other, "He saved others, but he cannot save himself! ³² Let us see the Messiah, the king of Israel, come down from the cross now, and we will believe in him!"

And the two who were crucified with Jesus insulted him also.

The Death of Jesus
(Matt. 27.45–56; Luke 23.44–49; John 19.28–30)

33 At noon the whole country was covered with darkness, which lasted for three hours. ³⁴ At three o'clock Jesus cried out with a loud shout, "*Eloi, Eloi,*

ˣ *Some manuscripts add verse 28:* In this way the scripture came true which says, "He shared the fate of criminals" *(see Lk 22.37).*

Aha! ...come down from the cross (15.29,30)

lema sabachthani?" which means, "My God, my God, why did you abandon me?"

35 Some of the people there heard him and said, "Listen, he is calling for Elijah!" 36 One of them ran up with a sponge, soaked it in cheap wine, and put it on the end of a stick. Then he held it up to Jesus' lips and said, "Wait! Let us see if Elijah is coming to bring him down from the cross!"

37 With a loud cry Jesus died.

38 The curtain hanging in the Temple was torn in two, from top to bottom. 39 The army officer who was standing there in front of the cross saw how Jesus had died.*y* "This man was really the Son of God!" he said.

40 Some women were there, looking on from a distance. Among them were Mary Magdalene, Mary the

*y*had died; *some manuscripts have* had cried out and died.

mother of the younger James and of Joseph, and
Salome. 41They had followed Jesus while he was in
Galilee and had helped him. Many other women who
had come to Jerusalem with him were there also.

The Burial of Jesus
(Matt. 27.57–61; Luke 23.50–56; John 19.38–42)

42-43 It was towards evening when Joseph of
Arimathea arrived. He was a respected member of
the Council, who was waiting for the coming of the
Kingdom of God. It was Preparation day (that is,
the day before the Sabbath), so Joseph went boldly
into the presence of Pilate and asked him for the
body of Jesus. 44Pilate was surprised to hear that
Jesus was already dead. He called the army officer
and asked him if Jesus had been dead a long time.
45After hearing the officer's report, Pilate told Joseph
he could have the body. 46Joseph bought a linen sheet,
took the body down, wrapped it in the sheet, and
placed it in a tomb which had been dug out of solid
rock. Then he rolled a large stone across the entrance
to the tomb. 47Mary Magdalene and Mary the mother
of Joseph were watching and saw where the body
of Jesus was placed.

The Resurrection
(Matt. 28.1–8; Luke 24.1–12; John 20.1–10)

16 After the Sabbath was over, Mary Magdalene,
Mary the mother of James, and Salome bought
spices to go and anoint the body of Jesus. 2Very
early on Sunday morning, at sunrise, they went to
the tomb. 3-4On the way they said to one another,
"Who will roll away the stone for us from the entrance
to the tomb?" (It was a very large stone.) Then they
looked up and saw that the stone had already been
rolled back. 5So they entered the tomb, where they
saw a young man sitting on the right, wearing a
white robe—and they were alarmed.

6 "Don't be alarmed," he said. "I know you are
looking for Jesus of Nazareth, who was crucified.
He is not here—he has been raised! Look, here is
the place where they put him. 7Now go and give
this message to his disciples, including Peter: 'He is

going to Galilee ahead of you; there you will see
him, just as he told you.' "

8 So they went out and ran from the tomb, distressed

So they went out and ran (16.8)

and terrified. They said nothing to anyone, because
they were afraid.

AN OLD ENDING TO THE GOSPEL z
Jesus Appears to Mary Magdalene
(Matt. 28.9–10; John 20.11–18)

[9 After Jesus rose from death early on Sunday, he
appeared first to Mary Magdalene, from whom he
had driven out seven demons. 10 She went and told
his companions. They were mourning and crying; 11 and
when they heard her say that Jesus was alive and
that she had seen him, they did not believe her.

Jesus Appears to Two Disciples
(Luke 24.13–35)

12 After this, Jesus appeared in a different manner
to two of them while they were on their way to
the country. 13 They returned and told the others, but
they would not believe it.

z *Some manuscripts and ancient translations do not have this
ending to the Gospel (verses 9–20).*

Jesus Appears to the Eleven
(Matt. 28.16–20; Luke 24.36–49; John 20.19–23; Acts 1.6–8)

14 Last of all, Jesus appeared to the eleven disciples as they were eating. He scolded them, because they did not have faith and because they were too stubborn to believe those who had seen him alive. 15 He said to them, "Go throughout the whole world and preach the gospel to all mankind. 16 Whoever believes and is baptized will be saved; whoever does not believe will be condemned. 17 Believers will be given the power to perform miracles: they will drive out demons in my name; they will speak in strange tongues; 18 if they pick up snakes or drink any poison, they will not be harmed; they will place their hands on sick people, who will get well."

Jesus Is Taken up to Heaven
(Luke 24.50–53; Acts 1.9–11)

19 After the Lord Jesus had talked with them, he was taken up to heaven and sat at the right side of God. 20 The disciples went and preached everywhere, and the Lord worked with them and proved that their preaching was true by the miracles that were performed.]

ANOTHER OLD ENDING [a]

[9 The women went to Peter and his friends and gave them a brief account of all they had been told. 10 After this, Jesus himself sent out through his disciples from the east to the west the sacred and ever-living message of eternal salvation.]

---

[a] Some manuscripts and ancient translations have this shorter ending to the Gospel in addition to the longer ending (verses 9–20).

58

Some stories from the Good News

page

Some of Jesus' Parables

Some of Jesus' Miracles page

What to read when you are feeling: